Y0-CBI-182

Irish Americans

Edited by
Kem Knapp Sawyer

*Irish domestics, around 1870, were referred to as "Brigets" and
"Kathleens." (Courtesy of the State Historical Society of Wisconsin)*

Discovery Enterprises, Ltd.
Carlisle, Massachusetts

© Discovery Enterprises, Ltd., Carlisle, MA 1998

ISBN 1-57960-028-X paperback edition
Library of Congress Catalog Card Number 97-77594

10 9 8 7 6 5 4 3 2 1

Printed in the United States of America

Subject Reference Guide:

Irish Americans
Edited by Kem Knapp Sawyer

Irish Immigration to America — U.S. History

Irish Americans — U.S. History

Credits:

Cover illustration: Irish emigrants leaving home — the priest's blessing
(The Illustrated London News, 10 May 1851)

Illustrations cited where they appear in the text.

Editor's notes regarding the documents:

1. *All original spelling has been retained.*

2. *A full line of dots indicates the deletion of at least an entire paragraph.*

Table of Contents

Introduction

by Kem Knapp Sawyer

For centuries the Irish crossed the Atlantic to come to the United States in pursuit of new opportunities — work, prosperity, and freedom. Many, hungry and penniless when they left Ireland, sought jobs and the means to feed their families. Some, jailed or denied property rights for their religious beliefs, hoped to find a community where religious tolerance prevailed. Others came to join family, to seek adventure, or to improve their lot.

Looking back, we can trace the arrival of the first Irishman to the voyage of Christopher Columbus in 1492. Among the forty-two men who sailed the *Santa Maria* was listed one "William from Galway." Also aboard the ship was an Irish wolfhound. Later, as Great Britain established colonies in the New World, the Irish joined other emigrants in the journey across the ocean.

The political unrest at home made many Irish eager to leave, while others were sent against their will. Tension between Protestants and Catholics mounted and resulted in several rebellions. In the 1640s, England's ruler, Oliver Cromwell, suppressed the Irish, killing thousands and transporting 100,000 to America. Many of these political prisoners were taken to the West Indies, later finding their way north to Massachusetts. At the Battle of the Boyne in 1690 the Catholics, led by the exiled King James II, were defeated by King William's Protestant army. William III enforced cruel Penal Laws, taking away the rights of Catholics to vote, sit in Parliament, join the army, purchase property, or carry a sword. He closed churches and schools across the land. The priests who secretly ran their own schools did so knowing they put their lives at risk. The Penal Laws affected not only Catholics, but also Presbyterians — the Protestants who had moved from Scotland to northern Ireland.

During the eighteenth century 250,000 Irish, both Catholic and Protestant, found refuge in America. The first wave of immigrants was Presbyterian, often called Scotch-Irish, and was later followed by Catholic emigrants. After the American Revolution, when the new republic repealed many of the anti-Catholic laws enforced by the British, Catholics began to emigrate in greater numbers. Many were poor and had lost their land. Some came as indentured servants, offering their services to a master who would pay their way. Others paid their own way and found jobs as kitchen maids, apprentices, shopkeepers or schoolmasters.

Irish children searching for potatoes in West Cork. (Illustrated London News, *20 Feb. 1847)*

Immigration continued at a steady pace until 1845 when a terrible famine occurred in Ireland and her people, hungry and desperate, fled in droves. A potato blight ruined the crop that fed a nation. One million Irish died of starvation and related diseases. The population declined even more drastically as huge numbers, 1,500,000, came to America. In six years 5,000 ships made the 3,000 mile journey across the Atlantic with passengers crammed into tight, airless spaces where sanitary conditions were dreadful and disease rampant. So many died along way that the vessels took on the name of 'coffin ships.' One such ship, the *Elizabeth and Sarah*, built in 1762 to accommodate 155 persons, sailed from County Mayo in 1846 with 276 persons. The sleeping berths were in such disrepair that only thirty-six could be used and most passengers slept on the floor. She should have stored 12,532 gallons of water, but only carried 8,700 gallons. Forty-two persons died during the voyage.

The new immigrants flocked towards large cities, such as Boston, New York, Philadelphia, Savannah, Chicago and St. Louis, where many found homes in tenements in Irish neighborhoods. But whether poor or 'lace curtain' (as the more well-to-do were called), the Irish, now mostly Catholic, had to contend with prejudice. Job discrimination occurred routinely with the words "No Irish Need Apply" posted on many a job notice. Yet, as the decades passed, the burden of discrimination decreased; Irish Americans became more accepted into the mainstream without losing their identity. During the Civil War a large number of "potato famine immigrants" were quick to join the Union army. As many as 144,221 men, one fourth of the foreign born volunteers, came from Ireland. New York's renowned "Fighting Sixty-ninth" and other regiments banded together to form the Irish Brigade, fighting bravely at the battles of Antietam and Fredericksburg, where many Irish sacrificed their lives.

Recruiting poster for an Irish Brigade
(Courtesy of the Library of Congress)

Throughout the nineteenth century the working class Irish helped build the nation by working in factories and mines, building roads, digging canals and laying tracks. But many of their dreams for achieving prosperity in America were dashed when they were confronted with appalling working conditions: low wages, long hours, child labor, no paid holidays. Sickness or child-birth resulted in the loss of a job and an uncertain future. Many Irish Americans became leaders in the labor movement, organizing trade unions and campaigning for more humane work practices. In 1879, Terence V. Powderley was elected head (or "grand master workman") of the Knights of Labor, the first major national labor organization, and other Irish Americans followed suit. The Irish also formed a loyal allegiance to the Democrats and more often than not ruled city politics. James Michael Curley took control of Boston and Thomas J. Pendergast did the same in Kansas City. Both were colorful, popular, and powerful bosses who tried to please the working classes; but they also contributed to the image of corruption big city politics had earned.

New York City politics were run by Tammany Hall, a core group of the Democratic party with a sizable Irish component, among them "Honest John" Kelly who ruled from 1872 to 1886. Tammany Hall's Al Smith, four-time governor from New York, became the first Catholic to run for president. The Democratic nominee in 1928, he was defeated by Herbert Hoover. Although Irish Catholics held many important political offices, none was elected to the presidency until 1960, when John F. Kennedy, the great grandson of an Irish immigrant, would become the first Catholic president.

The contributions of Irish Americans to the arts have been enor-mous and include the Civil War photographer Mathew Brady; the painter Georgia O'Keefe; the First Lady of American Theater, Helen Hayes; the musical comedy playwright George M. Cohan, who gave us "Yankee Doodle Dandy" and "Give my Regards to Broadway." Eugene O'Neill, who tells the story of his own Irish family in the master-piece *Long Day's Journey into Night,* is the only playwright to have won the Nobel Prize for literature. He once told his son, "The critics have missed the important thing about me and my work, the fact that I am Irish." Many actors have graced both stage and screen, including Spencer Tracy, James Cagney, Maureen O'Sullivan, and Gene Kelly. Numerous authors, such as F. Scott Fitzgerald, John O'Hara, Flannery O'Connor, Mary McCarthy, and William Kennedy have written about the Irish American experience, often telling poignant stories with humor and wit. In 1996, Frank McCourt won the Pulitzer Prize for his Irish American memoirs, *Angela's Ashes*.

Over the course of the last three centuries, seven million people left Ireland for America. Today the United States can claim forty million Americans with Irish roots. Many care deeply for the heritage they wish to pass on to future generations. For some, the bond between the two countries has never been broken; they work hard to strengthen the ties. Northern Ireland has been in turmoil for the last thirty years with 3,200 people dying as a result of violence between Catholics and Protestants. Many Irish Americans have been drawn into that conflict as well, including Senator Edward Kennedy and Thomas P. "Tip" O'Neill, former Speaker of the House of Representatives, seeking a peaceful resolution. President Bill Clinton made this a priority of his administration. President Clinton, on a visit to Ireland in November 1995, addressed his Belfast audience:

> Irish Protestant and Irish Catholic together have added to America's strength. From our battle for independence down to the present day, the Irish have not only fought in our wars, they have built our Nation, and we owe you a very great debt. Let me say that of all the gifts we can offer in return, perhaps the most enduring and the most precious is the example of what is possible when people find unity and strength in their diversity.

Early Immigrants

This letter, written in 1789 by Phineas Bond, the British consul in Phila-delphia, to Lord Carmarthen, British secretary for foreign affairs, describes the arrival of some of Ireland's earliest immigrants. Many came as indentured servants, while others paid their own passage.

Source: *Annual Report of the American Historical Association*, 1896, I, pp. 643-645. Extract from Edith Abbott, *Immigration: Select Documents and Case Records*, The University of Chicago Press, 1924. Reprinted by New York: Arno Press, 1969, pp. 9-10.

Formerly, my Lord, a large portion of the passengers from Ireland were redemptioners or indented servants, those who could not redeem themselves by paying their passage money within a limited time were then indented for a term of years to any master who would advance the price of their passages — those who came out as servants were indented in Ireland for so many years to the master or owner of the vessel and the original indenture was either assigned or a new one given upon their arrival in America to the first person who would pay the price demanded for their time. The laws of Pennsylvania require certain freedom dues to be allowed by the master to the servant upon the expiration of the term of servitude. Lately, my Lord, few redemptioners or servants have arrived here from Ireland, the passengers from thence have been chiefly such as have paid their passage before they embarked; in this sort of trade there is very little risk and great profit, the passengers who have arrived in the Delaware this year from Ireland have been for the most part people in tolerable good plight with some property beforehand and who have come to settle as farmers or to engage as artificers in some branch of manufacture. A large embarkation of this description of pas-sengers as well as of redemptioners and servants is expected in the course of next year.

Irish Schoolmasters

When the Irish first set foot in the American colonies they took on a wide variety of jobs; a surprising number, however, became teachers. Many Catholic schoolmasters, banned from teaching in Ireland, sought refuge in America. Some were sent as political prisoners to the West Indies and later escaped to the colonies. Other schoolmasters fled to America before they were apprehended. These teachers opened schools in villages, tutored in homes, or traveled from one town to another to give lessons.

The following account, written in 1898, identifies many of the first Irish schoolmasters.

Source: John C. Linehan and Thomas Hamilton Murray, *Irish Schoolmasters in the American Colonies, 1640-1775*, Washington, D.C.: The American-Irish Historical Society, 1898, pp. 5-12.

Irish schoolmasters were numerous in the American Colonies long before the Revolution. For generations they imparted tuition and had the satisfaction of seeing great numbers of their pupils attain positions of eminence.

Many of the leading patriots of the Revolution were educated by Irish teachers, and regarded their instructors with respect and affection...

In 1640, William Collins accompanied a party of refugees from the West Indies to what is now New Haven, Conn. After a time, these refugees dispersed in various directions and some returned to Ireland. Collins taught school at Hartford for a period. There is very little doubt that he was Irish...

Thomas Dongan, son of an Irish baronet, was appointed governor of New York in 1683. He was a wise, humane and just man and did much to encourage education. During his administration a Catholic college was opened in New York, by two or three Catholic clergymen, with an admirable course of studies. Many other Catholic teachers, of Irish and other nationalities, are heard from in Colonial days.

Peter Pelham started a school in Boston as early as 1734. He was one of the Protestants who founded the Charitable Irish Society of that city and is described as "of the Irish Nation residing in Boston." In 1737 an application to the selectmen appears from him for "Liberty to open a School in this Town for the Education of Children in Reading, Writing, Needle-work, Dancing and the Art of Painting upon Glass, etc." His application was granted.

Robert Alexander, with his brothers Archibald and William, came here from Ireland about 1736, and may justly be considered the founder of Washington and Lee University, Virginia. Robert started a school in 1749 which was known as Augusta Academy until 1776; from the latter year until 1798 it was called Liberty Hall Academy; from 1798 to 1813 it was styled Washington Academy; from 1813 to 1871 it was Washington College, and in 1871 it received its present title — Washington and Lee University...

Wall, an Irishman, was the first teacher in the school established by Sir William Johnson in the Mohawk Valley. Johnson was born in Meath county, Ireland, in 1715. He treated the Indians kindly and honestly, was adopted into the Mohawk tribe and was made a sachem [supreme leader]. In 1775, at a council of governors convened by Braddock, Johnson was designated as "sole superintendent of the Six Nations."

...Charles Thomson, an Irishman, was born in 1729. He came to this country with his three sisters in 1741 and was educated by the distinguished Rev. Dr. Alison. Thomson became a teacher in Philadelphia and at the Friends' school at New Castle, Del. He was permanent secretary of the Continental Congress, and was a sterling patriot. The Indians had great admiration for Thomson and referred to him as "one who speaks the truth."

...Rev. Samuel Finley, D.D., who became President of the College of New Jersey, 1761, was an Irishman, a native of Armagh, born in 1715. He came with his parents to America in 1734, and later established an academy at Nottingham, Md., which soon obtained a great reputation for the excellence of the instruction given. Dr. Sprague declared of Finley that "he was an accomplished teacher, and among his pupils were some of the very best scholars of the day. He boarded most of them in his own house and at his table." Under President Finley, the College of New Jersey made rapid progress...

Robert Adrain, an Irishman, was another prominent American educator. He was born in Carrickfergus, Sept. 30, 1775. He became a member of the Society of United Irishmen and participated in the Irish revolt of 1798. He was a school-teacher in his sixteenth year. In the outbreak of 1798, just mentioned, Adrain had command of a company, and the English offered a reward of 50 pounds for his capture. He escaped, however, and came to the United States. He taught in an academy located at Princeton, N.J.; became principal of York County Academy, Pa.; had charge of an academy in Reading, Pa.; was made Professor of Mathematics and Natural Philosophy in what is now Rutgers College; became professor of the same branches in Columbia College, New York, and was later Vice-Provost of the University of Pennsylvania...

The foregoing are but a few of the host of educators Ireland gave this country in the days gone by.

Letter from John Doyle to his Wife

Health and economic circumstances often made it impractical, if not impossible, for families to emigrate together. This letter, dated January 25, 1818, is written by John Doyle, an Irish immigrant in New York City, to his wife in Ireland.

Source: William D. Griffin, *The Book of Irish Americans*, New York: Times Books, 1990, pp. 119-120.

Oh, how long the days, how cheerless and fatiguing the nights since I parted with my Fanny and my little angel. Sea sickness, nor the toils of the ocean, nor the starvation which I suffered, nor the constant apprehension of our crazy old vessel going to the bottom, for ten tedious weeks, could ever wear me to the pitch it has if my mind was easy about you. But when the recollection of you and of my little Ned rushes on my mind with a force irresistible, I am amazed and con-founded to think of the coolness with which I used to calcu-late on parting with my little family even for a day, to come to this strange country, which is the grave of the reputations, the morals, and of the lives of so many of our countrymen and countrywomen...

We were safely landed in Philadelphia on the 7th of October and I had not so much as would pay my passage in a boat to take me ashore... I, however, contrived to get over, and...it was not long until I made out my father, whom I instantly knew, and no one could describe our feelings when I made myself known to him, and received his embraces, after an absence of seventeen years... The morning after landing I went to work to the printing... I think a journeyman printer's wages might be averaged at 7 1/2 dollars a week all the year round... I worked in Philadelphia five and one-half weeks and saved 6 pounds, that is counting four dollars to the pound...

As yet it's only natural I should feel lonesome in this country, ninety-nine out of every hundred who come to it are at first disappointed... Still, it's a fine country and a much better place for a poor man than Ireland...and much as they grumble at first, after a while they never think of leaving it... One thing I think is certain, that if emigrants knew beforehand what they have to suffer for about the first six months after leaving home in every respect, they would never come here. However, an enterprising man, desirous of advancing himself in the world, will despise everything for coming to this free country, where a man is allowed to thrive and flourish without having a penny taken out of his pocket by government; to act and speak as he likes, provided he does not hurt another, to slander and damn government, abuse public men in their office to their faces, wear your hat in court and smoke a cigar while speaking to the judge as familiarly as if he was a common mechanic, hundreds go unpunished for crimes for which they would be surely hung in Ireland; in fact they are so tender of life in this country that a person should have a very great interest to get himself hanged for anything.

The Irish Emigrant Ballad

The Irish brought to America a great love of music. Many of the early Irish ballads refer to the hopes and dreams of the emigrants as well as the severe hardships they encountered on their journeys. In this ballad the emigrant remembers the one he left behind.

Source: Robert L. Wright, ed., *Irish Emigrant Ballads and Songs*, Bowling Green, Ohio: Bowling Green University Popular Press, 1975, p. 254.

Oh I'm sitting on the stile, Mary, where we sat side by side,
On a bright May morning long ago when first you were my bride;
The corn was springing fresh and green and the lark sang loud
and high,
And the red was on your lips, Mary, and the love lay in your eye.

The place is little changed, Mary, the day is right as then,
The lark's loud song is in my ear and the corn is green again;
But I miss the softness of your hand and your breath warm
on my cheek,
And I still keep listening for the words you never more will speak.

'Tis but a step down yonder lane, the little church stands near,
The place where we were wed, Mary, I see the spire from here;
And the grave-yard stands between us both where you took
your final rest,
Where I laid you, darling, down to sleep with your babe all on
your breast.

I'm very lonely now, Mary, for the poor make no new friends,
But oh they love the better still the few our Father sends;
And you were all I had, Mary, my blessing and my pride,
There's nothing else to care for now since my poor Mary died.

I'm bidding you a long farewell, my Mary kind and true,
But I'll not forget you, darling, in that land I'm going to;
For they say there's bread and work for all and the sun shines
always there,
But I'll ne'er forget my Mary were it fifty times as fair.

Black '47

From 1845 to 1851 Ireland suffered from a terrible famine. The potato crop, on which much of the population depended almost exclusively for nourishment, had failed. The people most affected by the famine were not landowners, but tenant farmers who could no longer afford to pay the rent. As the landlords evicted them, they became homeless as well as hungry. These passages from the diary of one Irish schoolteacher, Gerald Keegan, describe life in Ireland during the famine, the temptation to emigrate, and the difficulties in making that choice. The year is 1847, one of the worst in Irish history, known to this day as Black '47.

Source: Gerald Keegan, *Famine Diary: Journey to a New World*, Dublin: Wolfhound Press. First published in 1895; reprinted in 1991.

February 18. I am beginning this journal today in the hope that it will be a message to the world from this downtrodden land of ours. I realize that it may never be beyond the confines of this little village in County Sligo. In that case I will at least have the satisfaction of putting my thoughts into words. They are the words of a poor village schoolmaster, one of the two thousand tenants on Lord Palmerston's huge estate.

If the outside world only knew the facts about Ireland's condition I know that we would get help. The news that is getting out, mainly from the *London Times*, is a complete distortion of what is actually going on. I am determined to write down everything that strikes me as the reality of our situation.

The weather on this bleak, cold February day is in tune with the mood and the state of the people all over the land. What is most heartrending to me is the sad plight of the children.

Today when I told my cousin, Timmy O'Connor, to put out his hand for punishment for neglecting to do any work all week he said: "It's not that I meant it, sir. It's the belly gripe that I feel all the time and I can't do any work." The tears in his eyes overwhelmed me. I am shocked at myself for even thinking of any kind of punishment for neglect of duty. What is duty after all when people are literally tortured by the pangs of hunger? When school was out I slipped a penny into Timmy's hand to buy a scone at the baker's...

February 19. When I came to my boarding house after school today Mrs. Moriarty, my landlady, told me that my Uncle Jeremiah was coming over to see me. Poor man, he must be coming to ask for some help to keep Timmy and the two girls alive. But I won't have a shilling in my pocket till the board pays my quarterly salary, if indeed my allowance could be called a salary.

The drawn and haggard look of Jeremiah when he came to the door left me in no doubt about his own half-starved condition. Many of the parents in this area are starving themselves in an attempt to keep their children alive. I got Mrs. Moriarty to roast another herring and serve it to him with a cup of tea...

It turned out that he did not come to borrow or beg but to talk of emigration. He claimed that the whole country was in the throes of a mass emigration movement to Canada. I knew about it myself but I also know that it is, deep down, a forced expulsion under a plan conceived and now being executed by the landlords...

February 21. It is true that there is a potato famine in practically every part of the country but there is corn and wheat and meat and dairy products in abundance. For putting his hands on any of this, the tenant is liable to prison, even to execution or to exile...

February 23. Together with Tim Maloney, an ardent patriot, and few other friends, I have some regular sources of information. Between them and a few newspapers we come across, we are getting a picture of the reality of these dark days.

The most disheartening effect of the intense sufferings of the people is a kind of despair and a sense of hopelessness that they are beginning to show. The average Irishman is a lover of conversation, music, poetry and even of leprauchauns, so symbolic of the spirit world in which we like to roam. But all of these, together with the saving gift of seeing the humorous side to even the most desperate situation, is giving way to an alarming indifference to what fate has seemingly decreed for us...

March 3. I started school after Christmas with 23 pupils. This week there are 14 left. I don't think I can endure facing their pathetic-looking glances much longer. I am trying to teach them something about the various uses of numbers, though about the only practical calculating they can do is to count the number who are dying around them every day...

March 7. Father Tom noted my presence in Church and he sent an altar boy to ask me to come and see him. After a hearty greeting he led me to his humble presbytery for a cup of tea... We had a long chat about the emigration movement. We agreed that it would be better to meet death right here, in preference to submitting to the treacherous terms of the landlords.

We did not mention it but I've heard that there is a price on his head. I feel that this will be our last meeting. When told about my engagement to Eileen Shanahan he was genuinely pleased and favoured going ahead with the marriage, suggesting that it would be a small tribute to life in a world of death...

March 8. Evictions and tumblings are going on at a mad rate now. The tumblings are cruel. The brutality of the herds of marauders who are smashing down the humble cottages of the tenants knows no bounds. People are beaten, even killed, when they resist. They are given no time to remove their few belongings. Seldom are there any reasons given for the evictions. Living on a choice bit of land, not turning in enough crop to the landlord, being in arrears with the landlord's rent or the fees collected by the State Church — any of these can serve as excuses for the tumblers to demolish a cabin without warning...

March 9. I had a long chat with Eileen today. She came to the school and saw my woe-begone little group of scholars. Acutely aware as she is, of all that is going on, she still continues to radiate happiness. On the way home she expressed her complete agreement with my plan to close the school very soon.

The main topic of our conversation was the emigration movement. Should we join the emigrants or should we stay here? We both want to do something for our people and the choice is a difficult one to make. The vast majority of the tenants in this district have made the decision to risk emigration. They are our kith and kin. And once they sign a paper they will be at the mercy of the landlords and their agents. We feel that they are the ones who will be in great need for help. These considerations make us feel that we should join them. Eileen's father, the last of her family, is going to move to Limerick where some of his relatives live. He is in ill-health and feels that his term is short...

Eileen showed me a clipping from the *London Times* which shows how ridiculously ill-informed, or should I say deliberately blind, are the people who are mainly responsible for our condition. The clipping contained a news item which tells us that the Queen, on the basis of information given to her by ministers of the government, declared that there seems to be a "dearth of provisions in Ireland." If she had only declared that there is a "dearth of provisions for a few million who are under the heel of oppression and plenty of food for the chosen few," she would have been telling the truth...

March 11. Tomorrow is Thursday, the day I intend to close my school... I am packing my few books this evening and trying to brace myself for tomorrow. Eileen knows the way I feel about it all and she is coming to visit me tomorrow evening. We will make our final decision on the emigration question.

March 12. I sat at my desk in school for a long time after the children left today. It was with tears in my eyes that I told them they would have to stay home for a while, though I myself knew it was forever. The ordeal of witnessing them trying to say goodbye to me was crushing. Some of them seemed to know that it was a final goodbye...

Eileen arrived early and, to get our minds off the present, we talked about our immediate future. If we are to join our people in their exodus we must get things done immediately. March 25 is our choice for a wedding date. Getting our few belongings together will be a simple matter for we own very little of this world's goods...

I was not at all surprised when Tim Maloney dropped in this evening. He keeps steady on the move and is finely tuned to what is really happening in these dark times. As usual he brought some important news. Referring to the emigrants he told us that the landlords have selected the old, the infirm, the children and the destitute for the first shiploads to Canada. Anyone who is still able to work for them, to make the land produce, they are trying to hold back...

March 13. The outside world is finally learning about our plight. Contributions are coming in. Newspapers in Dublin and Cork are publishing the names of countries, all over the world, that are collecting money and sending it here to help provide food for the starving. This is very uplifting. The thought that the outside world is concerned about us adds hope where all else is despair...

The United States, the chosen homeland of many thousands

of Irish emigrants, outdid all others in generosity. A city named Philadelphia topped all other United States centres in the magnitude of its donation. The Jewish people of New York City matched the Irish in their response to a public appeal for funds. Among all the donations from various parts of the world there is one that is singularly appreciated. It comes from a small tribe of native North American Indians, the Chocktaw tribe from central western United States. These noble-minded people, sometimes called savages by those who wantonly released death and destruction among them, raised money from their meagre resources to help the starving in this country. This is indeed the most touching of all the acts of generosity that our condition has inspired among nations...

March 16. The emigration scheme, though fraudulent and treacherous, is serving one useful purpose. It is raising a flicker of hope in the hearts of many who would otherwise give up. Countless thousands are now ready to take the chance... Today the local agent came with an attorney who got the people to sign a paper... What they are signing is a release of all claims on their property and furniture and a promise to give the agent possession by April 10...

March 22. Patrick Michael Shanahan, Eileen's father, died during the night. Like myself Eileen is an orphan now. On account of the pestilence Patrick will have to buried without delay...

March 24. Tomorrow, Thursday, is still a big question mark. As far as we ourselves are concerned, I mean Eileen and myself, there is nothing to prevent us from going ahead with the wedding ceremony. But convention demands a reasonable period of mourning... I purposely spoke to several of my closest friends to sound out their opinion. They all seem to think that, considering the times in which we live, there would be nothing indelicate about carrying out our plan...

March 27. Thursday was our big day and it was indeed a big day for our guests. After the wedding Mass, Father Flynn invited all present to a meal at the schoolhouse at noon hour. Where it all came from I cannot for the life of me imagine but there before us was a huge pot of hot vegetable soup, scones, and even some cakes, fish and gallons of tea...

March 31. It is early morning as I write this last note before departing. We now join a huge army forced to leave their native land for the convenience of the rich and the powerful. The heavy morning mist is a fitting curtain for the final scene, the climax, of all our strivings against impossible odds.

Gerald and Eileen reached Dublin where they joined five hundred passengers aboard the Naparima, *a ship built to hold three hundred. Many never made it to the New World. An outbreak of fever spread "like wildfire" among the passengers and crew. When the boat landed on Grosse Isle, an island on the St. Lawrence, Gerald and Eileen helped care for the sick, but the fever soon took their lives as well. Only Gerald Keegan's diary, entrusted to a priest on Grosse Isle, survived.*

'The Irish exodus' (A.M. Sullivan, The story of Ireland, Dublin, 1867.)

The Great Hunger

In The Great Hunger, *Cecil Woodham-Smith gives a history of the Irish famine and the political and economic circumstances that brought about the death of a million and a half people. Many emigrants who fled to America found passage on a ship bound not for the United States, but for Canada. Although the health and safety standards on these ships were minimal, the fares were substantially cheaper (often a third or a fourth the price) and therefore more attractive. Often ships sailing to the United States were booked, and the only passage available was to Quebec. Many of these emigrants eventually made their way to the United States, where they could escape British rule and find better economic opportunities.*

A typhus epidemic had occurred in Ireland; many passengers brought the highly contagious "ship fever" with them. Boats arriving in Quebec were required to stop for a medical inspection at Grosse Isle, an island on the St. Lawrence. The sick were at first sent to a quarantine hospital. But the huge numbers of people afflicted soon made a quarantine impossible to enforce.

Source: Cecil Woodham-Smith, *The Great Hunger*, London: Hamish Hamilton, 1962, pp. 230- 237.

For a modern interpretation of potato famine immigrants, see Andrea Barrett's *Ship Fever*, a short work of historical fiction that brings to life the suffering and determination of doctors and assistants who nursed the fever-ridden patients at Grosse Isle.

Meanwhile at Grosse Isle, by the middle of the summer of 1847, imposing a quarantine for fever had been abandoned as hopeless. The line of ships waiting for inspection was now several miles long; to make quarantine effective, twenty to twenty-five thousand contacts should be isolated, for whom there was no room on the small island. Therefore to carry out the quarantine regulations was, wrote Dr. Douglas, 'physically impossible,' and at the end of May passengers on ships with fever were allowed to stay, after the fever cases had been removed, and to perform their quarantine on board, the period to be fifteen days instead of ten. Dr. Douglas believed that a simple washing down and airing would make the holds healthy. 'After ablutions with water,' he wrote, 'by opening stern ports and bow ports...a complete current of air can pass through the hold, in fact a bird can fly through it.' So the passengers remained in the holds, with disastrous consequences.

So great was the number of sick that 'a fatal delay of several days' occurred before fever cases were taken away; meanwhile, sick and 'healthy' were cooped up together, and fresh infection took place. The *Agnes*, for instance, which arrived with 427 passengers, had only 150 alive after a quarantine of fifteen days.

Dr. Douglas was instructed to let the 'healthy' go from the ships without insisting on the full term of quarantine, and by the end of July quarantine had virtually been abandoned. A doctor came on board and inquired how many sick were below. He did not go into the hold, but placed himself at a table and called all emigrants able to walk to come up on deck; they filed past him, and anyone who seemed to him to be feverish was ordered to show his tongue. Those passed as 'healthy' were usually taken up to Montreal in a steamer, which picked up passengers at different vessels and had an appearance of gaiety because a fiddler and dancers were in the prow.

The journey up the St. Lawrence, from Grosse Isle to Montreal, took two to three days, and the emigrants were 'literally crammed on board the steamers, exposed to the cold night air and the burning sun...bringing the seeds of disease with them.' A number invariably developed fever on the way, and more than half had been known to arrive at Montreal in a dying condition.

On June 8 Dr. Douglas gave 'real fair warning to the authorities of Quebec and Montreal' that an epidemic was bound to occur: quarantine regulations were impossible to enforce, and the division between 'healthy' and sick was meaningless. Four thousand to five thousand so-called 'healthy' persons had left Grosse Isle on the previous Sunday; out of these, '2,000 at the least will fall sick somewhere before three weeks are over. They ought to have accommodation for 2,000 sick at least in Quebec and Montreal."

...By September, 1847, the date was not far distant when the St. Lawrence would be closed by ice; the last ships had left Britain in August, and the number of patients in hospital at Grosse Isle had at last begun to decrease. On September 13 the tents were struck, the church and the old passenger sheds, where patients had lain in rows on the floor, were fumigated, and the sick, now numbering about 1,200, sent to the new sheds which had at last been completed at the eastern end of the island. A fortnight later all convalescents were sent up to Point St. Charles. On October 21, when the first snow had already fallen, only sixty patients remained at Grosse Isle, and the authorities announced that the establishment would shortly be 'broken up.' On October 28, only two patients were left, and on the 30th Grosse Isle closed.

In a wooded hollow, one of the most beautiful of the miniature valleys of Grosse Isle, once the site of the emigrant cemetery, a four-sided monument commemorates those who died. On the first side the inscription runs:

> *In this secluded spot lie the mortal remains*
> *of 5,294 persons, who, flying from pestilence*
> *and famine in Ireland in the year 1847,*
> *found in America but a grave.*

A second side bears the names of Dr. Benson, of Dublin, and of three other doctors who died while attending the sick; the third, the names of two doctors who died on Grosse Isle during the cholera epidemic of 1832-34; and the fourth records that the monument was erected by Dr. Douglas and eighteen medical assistants who were on duty during the epidemic of 1847.

Famine Relief

In A Death-Dealing Famine, *Dr. Christine Kinealy, an Irish historian, questions why a study of the famine has been largely neglected over the last one hundred and fifty years. Her work provides new information as well as a balanced view of various historical interpretations of the famine. In this passage she discusses diverse forms of relief stemming from the United States.*

Source: Christine Kinealy, *A Death-Dealing Famine: The Great Hunger in Ireland*, London: Pluto Press, 1997, pp. 106-116.

An important although sometimes overlooked aspect of relief provision was the amount of money, food and other items provided by private charity for Ireland. The practice of raising private subscriptions during a period of food shortages was traditional. However, the scale and geographical scope of contributions provided during the Irish Famine was unprecedented.

The first international donation came from Calcutta at the end of 1845, as a result of a fund-raising initiative by members of the British army, many of whom were Irish-born... Concurrently with subscriptions raised in India, thousands of miles away in Boston a fund-raising committee was organised. News of the potato blight had reached Boston in November 1845. At the instigation of the Boston Repeal Association, a charitable fund was established, making it the first formal fund-raising structure in the United States...

By November 1846 tragic stories of starvation were appearing in the American press and were being reinforced by private letters sent from friends and family in Ireland. The circular sent by the Society of Friends in Dublin at the end of 1846 was widely publicised and used as a basis for fund-raising activities by non-Quakers throughout North America. The respect for the Quakers and their first-hand accounts from the west of Ireland led to a new wave of sympathy. In New York, a meeting in Tammany Hall raised 800 dollars and acted as a spur to other organisations to contribute the proceeds of social events. The seriousness of the Irish situation overcame much traditional native hostility to Ireland and to Catholics, which had been evident in 1846 when the president of an Irish Protestant organisation was jeered by his members for having given money to a Catholic fund. Instead, the main division emerged between those who believed that the Famine arose from British mismanagment and those who supported the response of the government.

The *Tribune* newspaper actively sought to encourage the inhabitants of New York to do more for Ireland, optimistically suggesting that 'the more unfeeling portion of the aristocracy of Ireland and Britain would feel rebuked and humbled by this exhibition of trans-Atlantic benevolence; they would be impelled to take effectual measures to prevent a recurrence of the occasion for it.' This did not prove to be the case. The Prime Minister, Lord John Russell, personally thanked the inhabitants of the United States for their generosity and allowed the removal of freight charges on charitable goods imported from the United States...

By February 1847, the cities of New York, Philadelphia and Baltimore had raised over one million dollars and collections were continuing. Again, as in the previous year, the trade of the United States was benefiting from the food shortages throughout Europe. Their generosity was also helped by the fact that America had enjoyed a bumper food harvest in 1846 and therefore had a considerable agricultural surplus...

Congress demonstrated its desire to help Ireland when, responding to a request by the Boston Relief Committee, it gave permission for the sloop of war the *Jamestown*...to be used to transport supplies to Ireland... This was a remarkable gesture in view of the fact that the United States was at war with Mexico, but the relief committees justified the action on the grounds that there was a critical shortage of seaworthy vessels to transport the relief to Ireland.

The voyage of the *Jamestown* caused much excitement and received widespread publicity in Ireland and America. On 17 March 1847 (St. Patrick's Day), foodstuffs began to be loaded onto the *Jamestown*, which left Massachusetts on 28 March. The ship was manned by volunteers who slept in hammocks on deck in order to maximise room for supplies. The Captain, Robert Bennett Forbes, was well-respected and had extensive experience, especially in China. In response to criticisms that a government warship was being used for such a purpose, he responded, 'It is not an everyday matter to see a nation starving.'

The Jamestown took 15 days and 3 hours to arrive in Cork. There it was greeted by the Liverpool philanthropist, William Rathbone, who had agreed to help oversee the impartial distribution of relief. Forbes was anxious that the distribution be carried out speedily, arguing that if the relief could cross the Atlantic in 15 days, it should not take a further 15 to reach the poor. To Forbes' embarrassment, he was feted on his arrival and two public receptions were held in his honour. He noted with approval that the ladies in Cork 'do shake their hands like men'; their handshake was 'no formal touching of the tip ends of the fingers, chilling the heart, but a regular grip of feeling.'

"Resolution of the New York Legislature on the Regulation of Emigrant Ships"

During the six years of the potato famine, from 1845 to 1851, an average of 300 Irish disembarked daily in the New York harbor. The emigrant ships were crowded, poorly stocked, unsanitary, and often in disrepair. This resolution was passed on February 5, 1847 in an attempt to improve the conditions of the vessels.

Source: "Concurrent Resolution, February 5, 1847," *New York State Laws* (1847), p. 379. Extract from Edith Abbott, *Immigration: Select Documents and Case Records*, The University of Chicago Press, 1924. Reprinted by New York: Arno Press, 1969, pp. 28-29.

Whereas, The regulation of commerce between foreign countries and the United States belongs, by virtue of the Constitution, to the Congress of the latter; and

Whereas, From the increase of emigration within the last few years the transportation of steerage passengers from the nations of Europe to this country has become a large and lucrative branch of commerce, profitable in proportion to the number of persons who can be induced to take passage on board of each vessel employed in this trade; and

Whereas, Many inhumane persons, careless of the wants, the health, and comfort of their passengers and eager only for gain, are now engaged in such transportation; and

Whereas, Almost weekly some such vessel, swarming with human beings, arrives at our port, and the details of their sufferings arising from the crowded state of such vessel, the neglect of the master to see secured a sufficiency of provisions and water for the voyage, and the conveniences of preparing food, the inattention of such master to the cleanliness of the steerage and the comfort and health of the passengers, are shocking to our sense of humanity and disgraceful to any country possessing the power to prevent the recurrence of such enormities: Therefore

Resolved, That our Senators in Congress be instructed, and our Representatives requested, to use their best efforts to obtain the passage of a law limiting and defining the number of passengers for each vessel engaged in the transportation of passengers from any foreign country to the United States ...determining the quantity of provisions and water for each passenger on the voyage, securing the presence of a physician on shipboard...to prevent the great and crying evils which at present so often occur...

NOTICE TO PASSENGERS
FOR NEW YORK.

ALL PASSENGERS FOR THE SHIP

CHUSAN, of Belfast,

Captain SHERAR,

ARE requested to be in BELFAST on TUESDAY, the 18th instant, to go on Board, as she SAILS the first Fair Wind after.

Apply to

DAVID GRAINGER, Dunbar's Dock; or, to
SAMUEL M'CREA, Waring Street.

Belfast, 11th April, 1848. (568

Notice to Passengers from the Belfast Newsletter, *April 1848.*

Westward Ho! An Irish View of the Emigrant's Opportunities

Most Irish immigrants flocked to the cities on the East coast, where many had great difficulties finding good jobs or comfortable homes. Here in an article appearing on February 3, 1855 in the Citizen, *New York's Irish American weekly, the writer urges immigrants to seek better opportunities in the west.*

Source: *Citizen*, II (New York City, February 3, 1855), p. 73. Extract from Edith Abbott, *Historical Aspects of the Immigration Problem: Select Documents*, The University of Chicago Press, 1926. Reprinted by Arno Press, 1969, pp. 298-299.

Westward Ho! The great mistake that emigrants, particularly Irish emigrants, make, on arriving in this country is, that they remain in New York, and other Atlantic cities, till they are ruined, instead of proceeding at once to the Western country, where a virgin soil, teeming with plenty, invites them to its bosom. Here, from the inadequate protection afforded them by the Commissioners of emigration, they become the easy prey of runners, boarding-house keepers and other swindlers; and, when their last cent is gone, they are thrown into the street, to beg or starve or steal, for employment there is none... Had they continued their journey westward, without halting, many of them would be now enjoying the happiness of independence, "monarchs of all they surveyed, with none their right to dispute." Their children and their children's children would revel in the glories and the grandeur of nature...

What then is the duty of the unemployed or badly paid emigrants residing in New York, Philadelphia and Boston? To start at once for the West.

In connexion with this important subject, we would advert to a letter published by a gentleman in Staten Island, containing the results of a circular he addressed, through the newspapers, to the farmers last Fall, for information respecting the demand for labor, the rates of wages, the cost of board, and the prospect of a poor man becoming the owner of an estate.

This gentleman, whose name is Olmsted, states that he received eighty-eight replies from various districts in nineteen states, and that out of these there were only nine who did not ask for more laborers, and seventy-three replies say that instances of workmen becoming proprietors are frequent. Eighty-six out of the eighty-eight represent the employees of both sexes as sitting at the same table with the employers, the women dressing quite as well as the farmers' daughters, and all of them sure to get well married whenever they please.

In some of the villages four-fifths of the owners of the land were laborers. One or two years' service is sufficient to earn enough to enable them to purchase 80 to 100 acres of Government land, erect a house upon it, set up farming on their own hook, and employ the next new comers.

Mr. Olmsted has compiled, from the letters he received, a table of wages. In Iowa, $240 is given, in Michigan, $230, in Illinois, $220, in Wisconsin from $100 to $150, in Connecticut, $180, the highest in Northern States. In New York, wages range from $85 to $100. In all cases these prices are in addition to board...

To the West, then, ye starving sons of toil — to the West! where there is food for all, employment for all, and where for all there are happy homes and altars free.

"On the Kind of Persons Who Ought to Emigrate"

In 1873, Reverend Byrne wrote a book offering advice to Irish people who were considering emigration. Here he discusses the problems of acquiring a home in a large eastern city and recommends moving to a smaller town in the West or the South—the same advice that was offered in the previous article written almost twenty years earlier. He also cautions against emigration for "persons of a more advanced age."

Source: Rev. Stephen Byrne, *Irish Emigration to the United States: What It Has Been, And What It Is: Facts and Reflections especially addressed to Irish People intending to emigrate from their native land; and to those living in the large cities of Great Britain and of the United States*, New York: The Catholic Publication Society, 1873. Reprinted by New York: Arno Press, 1969. pp. 26-27.

Those who cannot acquire homes of their own in one part of the United States by honest industry, frugality, and sobriety, ought to go where they can. The difficulty of doing it in all large cities is increased tenfold, when the high rents and high prices of the common necessaries of life are considered. Thus, for instance, in the city of New York, no laborer or mechanic can get a decent room or two in a tenement-house under twelve or fifteen dollars a month...It is clear and undeniable that men of the same class have gone either to the smaller towns of the West and South, or to the country parts, and have acquired their own homes in every case in which steadiness in work and sobriety justified the hope of their doing so.

Speaking of emigration from the old countries of Europe, it is well to remark that young people, from the ages of fifteen to twenty-five, are entirely more calculated to succeed than persons of a more advanced age. The customs and manners of all countries and of every people are different; and old people, or even those of the middle state of life, are seldom so easily brought into the customs of strangers as young people. Besides, it is natural to suppose that the affections of persons somewhat advanced in years for their native place are much stronger than those of young people; and the rupture of the ties which bind them to home is consequently attended with more pain. I have known many an aged father and mother, who, although having the kindest and the best children in the world to greet their landing in America, rarely, if ever, became reconciled to their lot. The familiar scenes and associations of from fifty to seventy years are lost; and no amount of novelty in the change of circumstances can fill up the blank caused thereby in the affections of the heart. If it were not for the deep religious sentiment which seems to be inherent in our race, much more discontent and despondence would prevail...

Years later, social photographer Lewis Hine captured these children of Irish immigrants, Maude and Grace Daly, working as shrimp pickers in Mississippi. (1911)

Irish Seamstress

Although the majority of Irish stayed on the east coast during the nineteenth century, many did go west, and some as far as California. Yet all did not find the economic prosperity they had been promised. Here a young Irishwoman describes the difficulties of working in the garment industry before trade unions helped to improve working conditions and wages. She is speaking to the Colorado Labor Bureau in 1886.

Source: Colorado Bureau of Labor, *Biennial Report for the Year Ending in 1886*, p. 122. Reprinted in Hasia R. Diner, *Erin's Daughters in America: Irish Immigrant Women in the Nineteenth Century*, Baltimore: The Johns Hopkins University Press, 1983, p. 78.

My parents live in Ireland and are entirely dependent on myself and sisters for support. I served an apprenticeship of three months, seven years since. I have worked at the trade ever since. I am a good seamstress and work hard. I try but I can not make over $1 per day. I pay rent for machine, $2.50 per month. Am not able to afford to ride on street cars, therefore I have to walk, and if I happen to be one minute late, I have to walk up long flights of stairs and am not allowed to go on the elevator.

Mother Jones

Mary Harris Jones, an Irish emigrant born in Cork, Ireland, was teaching school in Memphis, Tennessee when she met and married George Jones, an iron molder and organizer of the Iron Molders Union. In 1867, she lost her four children and her husband to a yellow fever epidemic. She moved to Chicago to open a dressmaking business. After her establishment burned in the great Chicago fire of October 1871, she took on the cause of working people, joined the many Irish members of the Knights of Labor, and helped organize strikes. She campaigned for better working conditions in mines, mills, railways, and factories. An early daring activist and an outspoken public speaker, she became known as Mother Jones. This selection is taken from her autobiography, published in 1925.

Source: Mary Harris Jones, *The Autobiography of Mother Jones*. First published in 1925, reprinted in Chicago by the Charles H. Kerr Publishing Company in 1990, pp. 71-83.

In the spring of 1903 I went to Kensington, Pennsylvania, where seventy-five thousand textile workers were on strike. Of this number at least ten thousand were little children. The workers were striking for more pay and shorter hours. Every day little children came into Union Headquarters, some with their hands off, some with the thumb missing, some with their fingers off at the knuckle. They were stooped little things, round shouldered and skinny. Many of them were not over ten years of age, although the state law prohibited their working before they were twelve years of age.

The law was poorly enforced and the mothers of these children often swore falsely as to their children's age. In a single block in Kensington, fourteen women, mothers of twenty-two children all under twelve, explained it was a question of starvation or perjury. That the fathers had been killed or maimed at the mines.

I asked the newspaper men why they didn't publish the facts about child labor in Pennsylvania. They said they couldn't because the mill owners had stock in the papers.

"Well, I've got stock in these little children," said I, "and I'll arrange a little publicity."

We assembled a number of boys and girls one morning in Independence Park and from there we arranged to parade with banners to the court house where we would hold a meeting.

A great crowd gathered in the public square in front of the city hall. I put the little boys with their fingers off and hands crushed and maimed on a platform. I held up their mutilated hands and showed them to the crowd and made the statement that Philadelphia's mansions were built on the broken bones, the quivering hearts and drooping heads of these children. That their little lives went out to make wealth for others. That neither state or city officials paid any attention to these wrongs. That they did not care that these children were to be the future citizens of the nation.

The officials of the city hall were standing in the open windows. I held the little ones of the mills high up above the heads of the crowd and pointed to their puny arms and legs and hollow chests. They were light to lift.

I called upon the millionaire manufacturers to cease their moral murders, and I cried to the officials in the open windows opposite, "Some day the workers will take possession of your city hall, and when we do, no child will be sacrificed on the altar of profit."

The officials quickly closed the windows, just as they had closed their eyes and hearts...

These little children were striking for some of the freedom that childhood ought to have, and I decided that the children and I would go on a tour...

The children carried knapsacks on their backs in which was a knife and fork, a tin cup and plate. We took along a wash boiler in which to cook the food on the road. One little fellow had a drum and another had a fife. That was our band. We carried banners that said, "We want more schools and less hospitals." "We want time to play." "Prosperity is here. Where is ours?"

We started from Philadelphia where we held a great mass meeting. I decided to go with the children to see President Roosevelt to ask him to have Congress pass a law prohibiting the exploitation of childhood. I thought that President Roosevelt might see these mill children and compare them with his own little ones who were spending the summer on the seashore at Oyster Bay...

The children were very happy, having plenty to eat, taking baths in the brooks and rivers every day. I thought when the strike is over and they go back to the mills, they will never have another holiday like this. All along the line of march the farmers drove out to meet us with wagon loads of fruit and vegetables. Their wives brought the children clothes and money. The interurban trainmen would stop their trains and give us free rides...Everywhere we had meetings, showing up with living children, the horrors of child labor...

We marched down to Oyster Bay but the president refused to see us and he would not answer my letters. But our march had done its work. We had drawn the attention of the nation to the crime of child labor. And while the strike of the textile workers in Kensington was lost and the children driven back to work, not long afterward the Pennsylvania legislature passed a child labor law that sent thousands of children home from the mills, and kept thousands of others from entering the factory until they were fourteen years of age.

Great Irish American Sports Figures

Irish Americans can claim several heavyweight boxing champions — John Sullivan, a bareknuckles winner, Jim Corbett, Terry McGovern, Jack O'Brien, Jack Dempsey, and Gene Tunney. Irish American names have also filled the annals of baseball — New York Giants manager Mugsy McGraw, the Delahanty brothers, Philadelphia Athletics manager Connie Mack, and the great catcher Mickey Cochrane, to name but a few. Many became legends in the late nineteenth and early twentieth centuries and were elected to the Baseball Hall of Fame. Although several Irish-American ballplayers claimed they inspired the greatest baseball poem of all, Ernest Thayer's "Casey at the Bat," Casey is most likely a fictitious character. The Irish Americans who called themselves the original Casey (and also performed public readings of the poem) include Daniel M. Casey of the Phillies and the famous base runner Mike "King" Kelly.

Source: "Casey at the Bat" by Ernest L. Thayer first appeared in the *San Francisco Examiner* on June 3, 1888 and was reprinted by Franklin Watts in 1964.

Casey at the Bat
by
Ernest Thayer

The outlook wasn't brilliant for the Mudville nine that day;
The score stood four to two with but one inning more to play;
And then, when Cooney died at first, and Barrows did the same,
A sickly silence fell upon the patrons of the game.

A struggling few got up to go, in deep despair. The rest
Clung to that hope which "springs eternal in the human breast;"
The thought, If only Casey could but get a whack at that,
We'd put up even money now, with Casey at the bat.

But Flynn preceded Casey, as did also Jimmy Blake,
And the former was a lulu and the latter was a cake;
So, upon that stricken multitude grim melancholy sat,
For there seemed but little chance of Casey's getting to the bat.

But Flynn let drive a single, to the wonderment of all,
And Blake, the much despised, tore the cover off the ball,
And when the dust had lifted and men saw what had occurred,
There was Jimmy safe at second, and Flynn a-huggin' third.

Then from five thousand throats and more there rose a lusty yell,
It rumbled through the valley; it rattled in the dell;
It knocked upon the mountain and recoiled upon the flat,
For Casey, mighty Casey, was advancing to the bat.

There was ease in Casey's manner as he stepped into his place;
There was pride in Casey's bearing and a smile on Casey's face,
And when, responding to the cheers, he lightly doffed his hat,
No stranger in the crowd could doubt 'twas Casey at the bat.

Ten thousand eyes were on him as he rubbed his hands with dirt;
Five thousand tongues applauded when he wiped them on his shirt.
Then, while the writhing pitcher ground the ball into his hip,
Defiance gleamed in Casey's eye, a sneer curled Casey's lip.

And now the leather-covered sphere came hurtling through the air,
And Casey stood a-watching it in haughty grandeur there,
Close by the sturdy batsman the ball unheeded sped —
"That ain't my style," said Casey. "Strike one," the umpire said.

From the benches, black with people, there went up a muffled roar,
Like the beating of the storm — waves on a stern and distant shore.
"Kill him; kill the umpire!" shouted someone from the stand; —
And it's likely they'd have killed him had not Casey raised his hand.

With a smile of Christian charity great Casey's visage shone;
He stilled the rising tumult; he bade the game go on;
He signaled to the pitcher, and once more the spheroid flew;
But Casey still ignored it, and the umpire said, "Strike two."

"Fraud," cried the maddened thousands, and echo answered "Fraud,"
But one scornful look from Casey, and the multitude was awed.

They saw his face grow stern and cold; they saw his muscles strain,
And they knew that Casey wouldn't let that ball go by again.

The sneer is gone from Casey's lip; his teeth are clenched in hate;
He pounds with cruel violence his bat upon the plate.
And now the pitcher holds the ball, and now he lets it go,
And now the air is shattered by the force of Casey's blow.

Oh! somewhere in this favored land the sun is shining bright;
The band is playing somewhere, and somewhere hearts are light.
And somewhere men are laughing, and somewhere children shout;
But there is no joy in Mudville — mighty Casey has Struck Out.

CHAMPIONS OF AMERICA.

Baseball became extremely popular after the Civil War. Pictured above, the Brooklyn Atlantics were champions in 1861, '64 and '65. This photo of the "Champion Nine," by Charles H. Williamson, was a prototype of baseball cards which became commonplace in the 1880s. (Courtesy of the Library of Congress)

Al Smith and the New York Irish

By 1860, New York had become the largest Irish city in the world with an Irish-born population of 203,000 out of a total of 805,000. A few years later one third of the city was Irish-born. For generations to come, the Irish left their mark on the city's culture, its neighborhoods, and its politics. One of the most prominent of New York's Irish American politicians was Alfred E. Smith, elected governor for four terms between 1918 and 1928. Born in Manhattan's Lower East Side, Al Smith would become a champion of progressive democracy. Often pictured with a derby and a cigar, he earned the nickname Happy Warrior. He was the first Roman Catholic to run for president, as a serious contender in 1924 and as the Democratic nominee in 1928.

In April 1927, the Atlantic Monthly *published a letter by Charles C. Marshall challenging Al Smith's candidacy for the presidency on the grounds that his religious beliefs would conflict with "loyalty and devotion" to the United States. Excerpts from Governor Smith's reply in the May 1927 issue follow.*

Source: Alfred E. Smith, *Progressive Democracy: Addresses and State Papers of Alfred E. Smith*, with an introduction by Henry Moskowitz, New York: Harcourt, Brace and Company, 1928.

In your open letter to me in the April *Atlantic Monthly* you "impute" to American Catholics views which, if held by them, would leave open to question the loyalty and devotion to this country and its Constitution of more than twenty million American Catholic citizens...You put your questions to me in connection with my candidacy for the office of President of the United States...

Taking your letter as a whole and reducing it to commonplace English, you imply that there is conflict between religious loyalty to the Catholic faith and patriotic loyalty to the United States. Everything that has actually happened to me during my long public career leads me to know that no such thing as that is true. I have taken an oath of office in this State nineteen times. Each time I swore to defend and maintain the Constitution of the United States. All of this represents a period of public service in elective office almost continuous since 1903. I have never known any conflict between my official duties and my religious belief. No such conflict could exist. Certainly the people of this State recognize no such conflict. They have testified to my devotion to public duty by electing me to the highest office within their gift four times...

I summarize my creed as an American Catholic. I believe in the worship of God according to the faith and practice of the Roman Catholic Church. I recognize no power in the institutions of my Church to interfere with the operations of the Constitution of the United States or the enforcement of the law of the land. I believe in absolute freedom of conscience for all men and in equality of all churches, all sects, and all beliefs before the law as a matter of right and not as a matter of favor. I believe in the absolute separation of Church and State and in the strict enforcement of the provisions of the Constitution that Congress shall make no law respecting an establishment of religion or prohibiting the free exercise thereof. I believe that no tribunal of any church has any power to make any decree of any force in the law of the land, other than to establish the status of its own communicants within its own church. I believe in the support of the public school as one of the corner stones of American liberty. I believe in the right of every parent to choose whether his child shall be educated in the public school or in a religious school supported by those of his own faith. I believe in the principle of noninterference by this country in the internal affairs of other nations and that we should stand steadfastly against any such interference by whomsoever it may be urged. And I believe in the common brotherhood of man under the common fatherhood of God. In this spirit I join with fellow Americans of all creeds

in a fervent prayer that never again in this land will any public servant be challenged because of the faith in which he has
tried to walk humbly with God.

*The song "Sidewalks of New York," composed in 1894, became a favorite
among the Irish as well as a theme song used by Al Smith in his 1928 cam-
paign for president.*

Source: Theodore Raph, ed., *The American Song Treasury: 100 Favorites*, New York: Dover
Publications, Inc., 1964, pp. 240-243.

Sidewalks of New York

Down in front of Casey's old brown wooden stoop
On a summer's evening we formed a merry group
Boys and girls together we would sing and waltz
While Tony played the organ on the sidewalks of New York

Chorus:
East side, west side, all around the town
The tots sang "ring-a-rosie," "London Bridge is falling down"
Boys and girls together, me and Mamie O'Rourke
Tripped the light fantastic on the sidewalks of New York...

Things have changed since those times, some are up in "G"
Others they are wand'rers but they all feel just like me
They'd part with all they've got, could they once more walk
With their best girl and have a twirl on sidewalks of New York.

Margaret Mitchell and
Gone with the Wind

Margaret Mitchell was the author of the most popular novel of all time,
Gone With the Wind, *a Pulitzer Prize winner, set in the American South
during the Civil War and published in 1936. An Irish American, she based
the character of Gerald O'Hara on her own grandfather, Thomas Fitzgerald.
In this scene Gerald O'Hara tells his daughter Katie Scarlett that Tara, the
family plantation, will one day be hers:*

Source: Margaret Mitchell, *Gone With the Wind*, New York: The MacMillan Company,
1936, pp. 36, 420-421.

"Do you stand there, Scarlett O'Hara, and tell me that Tara
— that land — doesn't amount to anything?"

Scarlett nodded obstinately. Her heart was too sore to care
whether or not she put her father in a temper.

"Land is the only thing in the world that amounts to anything," he shouted, his thick, short arms making wide gestures
of indignation, "for 'tis the only thing in this world that lasts,
and don't you be forgetting it! 'Tis the only thing worth working for, worth fighting for — worth dying for."

"Oh, Pa," she said disgustedly, "you talk like an Irishman!"

"Have I ever been ashamed of it? No, 'tis proud I am. And
don't be forgetting that you are half Irish, Miss! And to anyone with a drop of Irish blood in them the land they live on is
like their mother. 'Tis ashamed of you I am this minute. I offer
you the most beautiful land in the world — saving County
Meath in the Old Country — and what do you do? You sniff!"

"But there, you're young. 'Twill come to you, this love of
land. There's no getting away from it, if you're Irish. You're just
a child and bothered about your beaux. When you're older,
you'll be seeing how 'tis..."

Scarlett leaves Tara, but returns in the midst of the Civil War:

She could not desert Tara; she belonged to the red acres far more than they could ever belong to her. Her roots went deep into the blood-colored soil and sucked up life, as did the cotton. She would stay at Tara and keep it...Of a sudden, the oft-told family tales to which she had listened since babyhood, listened half-bored, impatient and but partly comprehending, were crystal clear. Gerald, penniless, had raised Tara; Ellen had risen above some mysterious sorrow...There were the Scarletts who had fought with the Irish Volunteers for a free Ireland and been hanged for their pains and the O'Haras who died at the Boyne, battling to the end for what was theirs.

All had suffered crushing misfortunes and had not been crushed...They had not whined, they had fought. And when they died, they died spent but unquenched. All of those shadowy folks whose blood flowed in her veins seemed to move quietly in the moonlit room. And Scarlett was not surprised to see them, these kinsmen who had taken the worst that fate could send and hammered it into the best. Tara was her fate, her fight, and she must conquer it.

Memories of a Catholic Girlhood

Mary McCarthy is an intellectual writer with Irish roots, the author of
The Group *and* The Groves of Academe. *Her father's relatives emi-
grated from Ireland before the potato famine to escape Catholic persecution.
She became an orphan at the age of six and was brought up by her grandpar-
ents in Minneapolis. Like many other Irish-American authors, she delves
frequently into her relationship with the Catholic church. In* Memories of
a Catholic Girlhood, *she tells how she first embraced it and then rebelled
against it. In this passage, the author recalls her first communion. It was
customary to fast before attending mass.*

Source: Mary McCarthy, *Memories of a Catholic Girlhood*, New York: Harcourt, Brace
and World, 1957, pp. 22-24.

Looking back, I see that it was religion that saved me. Our
ugly church and parochial school provided me with my
only aesthetic outlet, in the words of the Mass and the litanies
and the old Latin hymns, in the Easter lilies around the altar,
rosaries, ornamented prayer books, votive lamps, holy cards
stamped in gold and decorated with flower wreaths and a
saint's picture. This side of Catholicism, much of it cheapened
and debased by mass production, was for me, nevertheless,
the equivalent of Gothic cathedrals and illuminated manu-
scripts and mystery plays. I threw myself into it with ardor,
this sensuous life, and when I was not dreaming that I was
going to grow up to marry the pretender to the throne of
France and win back his crown with him, I was dreaming of
being a Carmelite nun, cloistered and penitential...

One of the great moral crises of my life occurred on the
morning of my first Communion. I took a drink of water.
Unthinkingly, of course, for had it not been drilled into me
that the Host must be received fasting, on the penalty of

mortal sin? It was only a sip, but that made no difference, I knew. A sip was as bad as a gallon; I could not take Communion. And yet I had to. My Communion dress and veil and prayer book were laid out for me, and I was supposed to lead the girls' procession; John Klosick, in a white suit, would be leading the boys'. It seemed to me that I would be failing the school and my class, if, after all the rehearsals, I had to confess what I had done and drop out. The sisters would be angry; my guardians would be angry, having paid for the dress and veil. I thought of the procession without me in it, and I could not bear it. To make my first Communion later, in ordinary clothes, would not be the same. On the other hand, if I took my first Communion in a state of mortal sin, God would never forgive me; it would be a fatal beginning. I went through a ferocious struggle with my conscience, and all the while, I think, I knew the devil was going to prevail: I was going to take Communion, and only God and I would know the real facts."

A Tree Grows in Brooklyn

This is the story of Francie Nolan, the daughter of an Irishman, born in 1901 and raised in the Williamsburg slums of Brooklyn. Betty Smith's novel has become a classic and tells what it was like for many second generation immigrants who struggled to make ends meet. Here Francie recalls seeing her father, Johnny Nolan, at the Union Headquarters:

Source: Betty Smith, *A Tree Grows in Brooklyn*, New York: Harper & Row, 1943, pp. 32-34.

Francie thought of the Union Headquarters. One time she had gone there to bring him an apron and carfare to go to a job. She saw him sitting with some men. He wore his tuxedo all the time. It was the only suit he had. His black derby was cocked jauntily and he was smoking a cigar. He took his hat off and threw the cigar away when he saw Francie come in.

"My daughter," he said proudly. The waiters looked at the thin child in her ragged dress and then exchanged glances. They were different from Johnny Nolan. They had regular waiter jobs during the week and picked up extra money on Saturday night jobs. Johnny had no regular job. He worked at one-night places here and there...

Francie pulled her thoughts away from that day when she had visited the Union Headquarters. She listened to her father again. He was reminiscing.

"Take me. I'm nobody." Placidly, he lit up a nickel cigar. "My folks over from Ireland the year the potatoes gave out. Fellow ran a steamship company said he'd take my father to America — had a job waiting for him. Said he'd take the boat fare from his wages. So my father and mother came over.

"My father was like me — never held the one job long...My folks never knew how to read or write. I only got to the sixth grade myself — had to leave school when the old man died.

You kids are lucky. I'm going to see to it that you get through school."

"Yes, Papa."

"I was a boy of twelve then. I sang in saloons for the drunks and they threw pennies at me. Then I started working around saloons and restaurants...waiting on people..." He was quiet awhile with his thought.

"I always wanted to be a real singer, the kind that comes out on the stage all dressed up. But I didn't have no education and I didn't know the first way about how to start in being a stage singer. Mind your job, my mother told me. You don't know how lucky you are to have work, she said. So I drifted into the singing waiter business. It's not steady work. I'd be better off if I was just a plain waiter."

Angela's Ashes

Like A Tree Grows in Brooklyn, *the Pulitzer Prize winning memoirs of* Frank McCourt, *Angela's Ashes, tells of a family's struggle with poverty through the eyes of a child. Frank McCourt was born in New York, but his family moved back to Limerick, Ireland to seek their fortune. Though they are met with hunger, poverty, and sickness, Frank's father never stops telling his children they must do their bit for Ireland. At the age of nineteen, Frank returned to New York. He later became a teacher and a quintessential Irish American, raised on both continents. In this first passage, Frank is still a young boy in Limerick.*

Source: Frank McCourt, *Angela's Ashes*, New York: Scribner, 1996, pp. 184-185, 290, 356-357.

The Dominican church is just up Glentworth Street.

Bless me, Father, for I have sinned, it's a fortnight since my last confession. I tell him the usual sins and then, I stole fish and chips from a drunken man.

Why, my child?

I was hungry, Father.

And why were you hungry?

There was nothing in my belly, Father.

He says nothing and even though it's dark I know he's shaking his head. My dear child, why can't you go home and ask your mother for something?

Because she sent me out looking for my father in the pubs, Father, and I couldn't find him and she hasn't a scrap in the house because he's drinking the five pounds Grandpa sent from the North for the new baby and she's raging by the fire because I can't find my father.

I wonder if this priest is asleep because he's very quiet till he says, My child, I sit here. I hear the sins of the poor. I assign the penance. I bestow absolution. I should be on my knees washing their feet. Do you understand me, my child?

I tell him I do but I don't.

Go home, child. Pray for me.

No penance, Father?

No, my child.

I stole the fish and chips. I'm doomed.

You're forgiven. Go. Pray for me.

He blesses me in Latin, talks to himself in English and I wonder what I did to him...

I'm thirteen going on fourteen and it's June, the last month of school forever. Mam takes me to see the priest, Dr. Cowpar, about getting a job as a telegram boy. The supervisor in the post office, Mrs. O'Connell, says, Do you know how to cycle, and I lie that I do. She says I can't start till I'm fourteen so come back in August.

Mr. O'Halloran tells the class it's a disgrace that boys like McCourt, Clarke, Kennedy, have to hew wood and draw water. He is disgusted by this free and independent Ireland that keeps a class system foisted on us by the English, that we are throwing our talented children on the dungheap.

You must get out of this country, boys. Go to America, McCourt. Do you hear me?

I do, sir...

Frank is now nineteen. Both his father and his brother Malachy have gone to England to work.

I tell Mam I'm going in a few weeks and she cries. Michael says, Will we all go some day?

We will.

Alphie says, Will you send me a cowboy hat and a thing you throw that comes back to you?

Michael tells him that's a boomerang and you'd have to go all the way to Australia to get the likes of that, you can't get it in America.

Alphie says you get it in America yes you can and they argue about America and Australia and boomerangs till Mam says, For the love o'Jesus, yeer brother is leaving us and the two of ye are there squabbling over boomerangs. Will ye give over?

Mam says we'll have to have a bit of party the night before I go. They used to have parties in the old days when anyone would go to America, which was so far away the parties were called American wakes because the family never expected to see the departing one again in this life. She says 'tis a great pity Malachy can't come back from England but we'll be together in America someday with the help of God and His Blessed Mother.

John F. Kennedy in Dublin

In 1848, during the potato famine, Patrick Kennedy left County Wexford in Ireland and sailed to the United States. He settled in Taunton, Massachusetts where he found work in a textile mill. His great grandson was John F. Kennedy. While president, John Kennedy traveled to Ireland where he addressed the Parliament in Dublin on June 28, 1963. Here he pays tribute to the contributions of the Irish in the making of America.

Source: *Public Papers of the Presidents of the United States: John F. Kennedy*, January 1 to November 22, 1963, Washington: United States Government Printing Office, 1964, pp. 534-539.

Mr. Speaker, Prime Minister, Members of the Parliament:

I am grateful for your welcome and for that of your countrymen.

The 13th day of December, 1862, will be a day long remembered in American history. At Fredericksburg, Va., thousands of men fought and died on one of the bloodiest battlefields of the American Civil War. One of the most brilliant stories of that day was written by a band of 1200 men who went into battle wearing a green sprig in their hats. They bore a proud heritage and a special courage, given to those who had long fought for the cause of freedom. I am referring, of course, to the Irish Brigade. General Robert E. Lee, the great military leader of the southern confederate forces, said of this group of men after the battle, "The gallant stand which this bold brigade made on the heights of Fredericksburg is well known. Never were men so brave. They ennobled their race by their splendid gallantry on that desperate occasion. Their brilliant though hopeless assaults on our lines excited the hearty applause of our officers and soldiers."

Of the 1200 men who took part in that assault, 280 survived

the battle. The Irish Brigade was led into battle on that occasion by Brig. Gen. Thomas F. Meagher, who had participated in the unsuccessful Irish uprising of 1848, was captured by the British and sent in a prison ship to Australia, from whence he finally came to America. In the fall of 1862, after serving with distinction and gallantry in some of the toughest fighting of this most bloody struggle, the Irish Brigade was presented with a new set of flags. In the city ceremony, the city chamberlain gave them the motto, "The Union, our country, and Ireland Forever." Their old ones having been torn to shreds by bullets in previous battles, Capt. Richard McGee took possession of these flags on December 2d in New York City and arrived with them at the Battle of Fredericksburg and carried them in the battle. Today, in recognition of what these gallant Irishmen and what millions of other Irish have done for my country, and through the generosity of the "Fighting 69th," I would like to present one of these flags to the people of Ireland.

As you can see, gentlemen, the battle honors of the Brigade include Fredericksburg, Chancellorsville, Yorktown, Fair Oaks, Gaines Mill, Allen's Farm, Savage's Station, White Oak Bridge, Glendale, Malvern Hill, Antietam, Gettysburg, and Bristow Station.

I am deeply honored to be your guest in the Free parliament of a free Ireland. If this nation had achieved its present political and economic stature a century or so ago, my great grandfather might never have left New Ross, and I might, if fortunate, be sitting down there with you...

I am proud to be the first American President to visit Ireland during his term of office, proud to be addressing this distinguished assembly, and proud of the welcome you have given me. My presence and your welcome, however, only symbolize the many and the enduring links which have bound the Irish and the Americans since the earliest days.

Benjamin Franklin — the envoy of the American Revolution who was also born in Boston — was received by the Irish parliament in 1772. It was neither independent nor free from discrimination at the time, but Franklin reported its members "disposed to be friends of America." "By joining our interest with theirs," he said, "a more equitable treatment...might be obtained for both nations."

Our interests have been joined ever since. Franklin sent leaflets to Irish freedom fighters. O'Connell was influenced by Washington, and Emmet influenced Lincoln. Irish volunteers played so predominant a role in the American army that Lord Mountjoy lamented in the British parliament that "we have lost America through the Irish."

And so it is that our two nations, divided by distance, have been united by history. No people ever believed more deeply in the cause of Irish freedom than the people of the United States. And no country contributed more to building my own than your sons and daughters. They came to our shores in a mixture of hope and agony, and I would not underrate the difficulties of their course once they arrived in the United States. They left behind hearts, fields, and a nation yearning to be free. It is no wonder that James Joyce described the Atlantic as a bowl of bitter tears. And an earlier poet wrote, "They are going, going, going, and we cannot bid them stay."

But today this is no longer the country of hunger and famine that those emigrants left behind. It is not rich, and its progress is not yet complete; but it is, according to statistics, one of the best fed countries in the world. Nor is it any longer a country of persecution, political or religious. It is a free country, and that is why any American feels at home.

There are those who regard this history of past strife and exile as better forgotten. But, to use the phrase of Yeats, let us not casually reduce "that great past to a trouble of fools." For we need not feel the bitterness of the past to discover its meaning for the present and the future. And it is the present and the future of Ireland that today holds so much promise to my nation as well as to yours, and, indeed, to all mankind.

For the Ireland of 1963, one of the youngest nations and the oldest of civilizations, has discovered that the achievement of nationhood is not an end but a beginning. In the years since independence, you have undergone a new and peaceful revolution, transforming the face of this land while still holding to the old spiritual and cultural values...

I am glad, therefore, that Ireland is moving in the mainstream of current world events. For I sincerely believe that your future is as promising as your past is proud, and that your destiny lies not as a peaceful island in a sea of troubles, but as a maker and shaper of world peace...

This has never been a rich or powerful country, and yet, since earliest times, its influence on the world has been rich and powerful. No larger nation did more to keep Christianity and Western culture alive in their darkest centuries. No larger nation did more to spark the cause of independence in America, indeed, around the world. And no larger nation has ever provided the world with more literary and artistic genius.

This is an extraordinary country. George Bernard Shaw, speaking as an Irishman, summed up an approach to life: Other people, he said, "see things and...say: 'Why?'...But I dream things that never were — and I say: 'Why not?'"

It is that quality of the Irish — that remarkable combination of hope, confidence, and imagination — that is needed more than ever today. The problems of the world cannot possibly be solved by skeptics and cynics, whose horizons are limited by the obvious realities...

My friends: Ireland's hour has come. You have something to give to the world — and that is a future of peace with freedom.

President Clinton in Northern Ireland

When John Kennedy in 1963 said Ireland was no longer a "country of persecution, political or religious," he spoke too soon. Just six years later, in 1969, the "Troubles" of Northern Ireland began, as Irish Catholics there fought for independence from Great Britain and union with the Republic of Ireland. In 1994, a cease-fire occurred and hopes for successful negotiations ran high. In February 1995, representatives from Britain and the Republic of Ireland agreed on the "Framework Document" which outlined a peace plan for Northern Ireland.

President Bill Clinton visited Ireland later that year to show his support for the peace process. On November 30, 1995 he traveled to Northern Ireland and spoke to factory workers at the Mackie International textile machinery plant in Belfast.

Source: William J. Clinton, *Public Papers of the Presidents of the United States: William J. Clinton*, Washington, D. C: United States Government Printing Office, 1996.

...Many of you perhaps know that one in four of America's Presidents trace their roots to Ireland's shores, beginning with Andrew Jackson, the son of immigrants from Carrickfergus, to John Fitzgerald Kennedy, whose forebears came from County Wexford. I know I am only the latest in this time-honored tradition, but I'm proud to be the first sitting American President to make it back to Belfast.

At this holiday season all around the world, the promise of peace is in the air. The barriers of the cold war are giving way to a global village where communication and cooperation are the order of the day. From South Africa to the Middle East and now to troubled Bosnia, conflicts long thought impossible to solve are moving along the road to resolution. Once-bitter foes are clasping hands and changing history, and long-suffering people are moving closer to normal lives.

Peace, once a distant dream, is now making a real difference in everyday life in this land. Soldiers have left the streets of Belfast; many have gone home. People can go to the pub or the store without the burden of the search or the threat of a bomb. As barriers disappear along the border, families and communities divided for decades are becoming whole once more.

This year in Armagh on St. Patrick's Day, Protestant and Catholic children led the parade together for the first time since the Troubles began. A bystander's words marked the wonder of the occasion when he said, "Even the normal is beginning to seem normal."

...America salutes all the people of Northern Ireland who have shown the world in concrete ways that here the will for peace is now stronger than the weapons of war. With mixed sporting events encouraging competition on the playing field, not the battlefield, with women's support groups, literacy programs, job training centers that serve both communities, these and countless other initiatives bolster the foundations of peace as well.

Last year's cease-fire of the Irish Republican Army, joined by the combined Loyalist Military Command, marked a turning point in the history of Northern Ireland. Now is the time to sustain that momentum and lock in the gains of peace. Neither community wants to go back to the violence of the past. The children told us that today. Both parties must do their part to move this process forward now...

The United States will help to secure the tangible benefits of peace. Ours is the first American administration ever to support in the congress the International Fund for Ireland, which has become an engine for economic development and for reconciliation. We will continue to encourage trade and investment and to help end the cycle of unemployment.

We are proud to support Northern Ireland. You have given America a very great deal. Irish Protestant and Irish Catholic together have added to America's strength. From our battle for independence down to the present day, the Irish have not only fought in our wars, they have built our Nation, and we owe you a very great debt.

Let me say that of all the gifts we can offer in return, perhaps the most enduring and the most precious is the example of what is possible when people find unity and strength in their diversity. We know from our own experience even today how hard that is to do. After all, we fought a great Civil War over the issue of race and slavery in which hundreds of thousands of our people were killed.

Today, in one of our counties alone, in Los Angeles, there are over 150 different ethnic and racial groups represented. We know we can become stronger if we bridge our differences. But we learned in our own Civil War that has to begin with a change of heart...

It is so much easier to believe that our differences matter more than what we have in common. It is easier, but it is wrong. We all cherish family and faith, work and community. We all strive to live lives that are free and honest and responsible. We all want our children to grow up in a world where their talents are matched by their opportunities. And I believe those values are just as strong in County Londonderry as they are in Londonderry, New Hampshire; in Belfast, Northern Ireland, as in Belfast, Maine.

I am proud to be of Ulster Scots stock. I am proud to be also of Irish stock. I share these roots with millions and millions of Americans, now over 40 million Americans. And we rejoice at things being various, as Louis MacNeice once wrote. It is one of the things that makes America special.

Because our greatness flows from the wealth of our diversity as well as the strength of the ideals we share in common, we feel bound to support others around the world who seek to bridge their own divides. This is an important part of our country's mission on the eve of the 21st century, because we know that the chain of peace that protects us grows stronger with every new link that is forged...

Over the last 3 years, I have had the privilege of meeting with and closely listening to both Nationalists and Unionists from Northern Ireland. And I believe that the greatest struggle you face now is not between opposing ideas or opposing interests. The greatest struggle you face is between those who deep down inside are inclined to be peacemakers and those who deep down inside cannot yet embrace the cause of peace, between those who are in the ship of peace and those who are trying to sink it. Old habits die hard.

There will always be those who define the worth of their lives not by who they are but by what they are against. They will never escape the dead-end street of violence. But you, the vast majority, Protestant and Catholic alike, must not allow the ship of peace to sink on the rocks of old habits and hard grudges. You must stand firm against terror. You must say to those who still would use violence for political objectives, "You are the past. Your day is over. Violence has no place at the table of democracy and no role in the future of his land." By the same token, you must also be willing to say to those who renounce violence and who do take their own risks for peace that they are entitled to be full participants in the democratic process. Those who do show the courage to break with the past are entitled to their stake in the future...

We will stand with those who take risks for peace in Northern Ireland and around the world. I pledge that we will do all we can, through the International Fund for Ireland and in many other ways, to ease your load. If you walk down this path continually, you will not walk alone. We are entering an era of possibility unparalleled in all of human history. If you enter that era determined to build a new age of peace, the United States of America will proudly stand with you.

But at the end of the day, as with all free people, your future is for you to decide. Your destiny is for you to determine. Only you can decide between division and unity, between hard lives and high hopes. Only you can create a lasting peace. It takes courage to let go of familiar divisions. It takes faith to walk down a new road. But when we see the right gaze of these children, we know the risk is worth the reward.

I have been touched by the thousands of letters I have received from schoolchildren here, telling me what peace means to them. One young girl from Ballymena wrote, and I quote, "It is not easy to forgive and forget, especially for those who have lost a family member or a close friend. However, if people could look to the future with hope instead of the past with fear, we can only be moving in the right direction." I couldn't have said it nearly as well...

In a speech later that day, President Clinton referred to two children who had introduced him at the Mackie plant:

A lot of incredibly moving things have happened to us today, but I think to me, the most moving were the two children who stood and introduced me this morning in the Mackie plant in Belfast...The young boy who introduced me said that he studied with and played with people who were both Protestant and Catholic, and he'd almost gotten to the point where he couldn't tell the difference. A beautiful young girl who introduced me — that beautiful child — started off by saying what her Daddy did for a living, and then she said she lost her first Daddy in the Troubles. And she thought about it every day. It was the worst day of her life, and she couldn't stand another loss. The upside and the downside, and those children joined hands to introduce me. I felt almost as if my speech were superfluous.

Suggested Further Reading

Barrett, Andrea. *Ship Fever*. New York: W.W. Norton & Company, 1996.

Cooper, Brian E., ed. *The Irish American Almanac and Green Pages*. New York: Harper & Row, 1990.

Diner, Hasia R. *Erin's Daughters in America*. Baltimore: Johns Hopkins University Press, 1983.

Fitzgerald, F. Scott. *This Side of Paradise*. New York: Charles Scribner's Sons, 1920.

Griffin, William D. *The Book of Irish Americans*. New York: Times Books, 1990.

Jones, Mary Harris. *The Autobiography of Mother Jones*. Chicago: Charles H. Kerr Publishing Company. First published in 1925; reprinted in 1990.

Keegan, Gerald. *Famine Diary: Journey to a New World*. Dublin: Wolfhound Press. First published in 1895; reprinted in 1991.

Kinealy, Christine. *A Death-Dealing Famine: The Great Hunger in Ireland*. London: Pluto Press, 1997.

Laxton, Edward. *The Famine Ships: The Irish Exodus to America*. New York: Henry Holt and Company, 1996.

McCarthy, Mary. *Memories of a Catholic Girlhood*. New York: Harcourt, Brace and World, 1957.

McCourt, Frank. *Angela's Ashes*. New York: Scribner, 1996.

O'Neill, Eugene. *Long Day's Journey into Night*. New Haven: Yale University Press, 1956.

Smith, Betty. *A Tree Grows in Brooklyn*. New York: Harper & Row, 1943.

Watts, J. F. *The Irish Americans*. New York: Chelsea House Publishers, 1988.

Woodham-Smith, Cecil. *The Great Hunger*. London: Hamish Hamilton, 1962.

About the Editor

Kem Knapp Sawyer was born in New York City and moved to New Hampshire when she was fourteen. A graduate of Yale University, she has taught English and drama. She and her husband Jon, and their three daughters, Kate, Eve, and Ida, enjoy putting on plays, bicycling, and camping (by the sea, in the mountains, or at the foot of a pyramid). They live in Washington, D.C. with a dog named Luke.

Kem is the author of two biographies also published by Discovery Enterprises, Ltd. about strong and dedicated Quaker women: *Lucretia Mott: Friend of Justice* and *Marjory Stoneman Douglas: Guardian of the Everglades*, both of which are written for ages 9 to 14.

She is also the editor of *Pennsylvania Dutch: The Amish and The Mennonites*, from this *Perspectives on History Series.*